# Your Words

# Are Like

# Swords

astral projections, lucid dreams,
and places I've been

by

Brian A. Labrecque

This book contains astral projections I've traveled on, lucid dreams I've experienced, and places I've been.

It's up to the reader to decide which are which.

Also on video as

Your Words are Like Swords

~ the movie ~

available from

www.laser.yoga

This book is dedicated to the memory of

Paul Tahi Baker

Published by Labrecque Art and Film.

All Rights Reserved

2012 Labrecque Art and Film

www.laser.yoga

ISBN: 978-0615719672

cover art by xyue-mayx.deviantart.com

I have no words

why, why, why

this world wasn't done with you yet

Goodbye Paul Tahi

# LIFE AND DEATH AND THE HEALING GLOWING PASSAGE TREE

If I'm standing proud in a field full of chaos, how can I escape? If my pride is my death sentence, do I pull off and burn my clothes and burn my money and burn my mind and climb the highest marble staircase, past the magnetosphere, to leap to my freedom? Will you catch my naked burning body, will you wipe the ash and embers from my skin, will you speak for me and tell my mother I'm ok? And after you make love to my body and my soul slips away, please don't leave me here.

Take me to the healing glowing passage tree, in the terrible teal forest, wrap me in branches and bark and blades of weeds and everything else. Pray for my soul to the healer in the healing tree, beg her to pry my insides away from the 3rd dimension and onto her perfect symmetry, so I can live in the light of awareness forever.

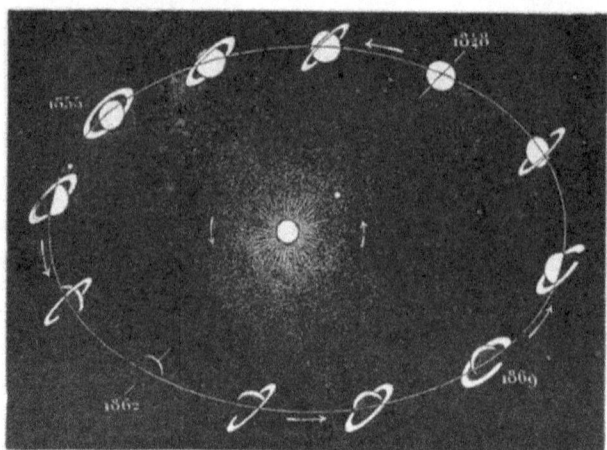

# 1. BLAZING STAR

Only transparent lines of frequency crossed my visual spectrum, distorting everything around me, at least from my point of view. Any peripheral noises in my house seemed muted, deadened and eventually silent, only a dusty green mist floated above me, which could have been a residual effect from my prior soul's life. Only this haze distracted me from those curly shapes floating like cotton balls from left to right, then right to left, across my face, and the threads never touched me. I could see the far wall of my bedroom through them. I tried to touch them, but they always moved away like squirrels, like scared squirrels.

I could feel a tingling, like pins and needles throughout the left side of my body, getting less intense by the second. I turned over, hoping the weight of my frame would increase the tingling, because I liked it... it did not. I suddenly started thinking about water and how much I hated it. How I didn't want to touch anything wet, or bright white or lit-up, that it would cause me searing pain if I did, the thought of everything being bright white, and wet and lit up and me being swallowed up by it would surly, at least in my mind, cause by body to melt into a wet runny batter. This, I knew, was a certainty. Glancing up to see if the green mist was still shining on me, it was, but, now turned to more of a bluish mist or cloud, which is a bit unnerving because typically I don't see anything floating above me, the mist was gone.

My eyes, and none other but my eyes, they suddenly release and now my mind is free, open, windy and dry, windows up, corn fields in view, dancing from the wind, as if they are celebrating your liberation with you.

I want to skip ahead to my future, like a smooth stone on a lake. When I say my future, I'm not talking about 10 years out, no, for me, just about 2 hours should be about the time I lose consciousness. I could call a hospital, but where's the fun in that? All they, the doctors and nurses, would do is to lecture me on the cons of killing myself. But what do they know? They're hypocrites, drowning in a sea of caustic gauze and plastic containers and colorful painkillers, they're the ones with a death wish, not me. I don't want to die, but the threat of dying in a couple hours makes me feel alive.

Maybe I need a plan in case things get out of hand and with a clear windy autumn brain, that's what I wanted.

I felt the same bunched up excitement that someone feels when they're about to eat the best meal ever, or meet the coolest person ever, that wondrous, awesome good-anxiety. When I drove up the on-ramp to the south freeway, it was dusk, the billboard lights were starting to light up, headlights were turning on all around me.

It was like Christmas.

My car radio didn't work, and one would think, at a time like this, I would want a soundtrack to this event, but I didn't need one, not from the radio anyways. I could hear a symphony all around me, singing to me in pitches and hues more beautiful than any I have ever heard.

The engine humming a soothing background to the wind noise, then there's the road sound, the tires playing the pavement like a musician would strike a violin. All this punctuated by the ebb and flow of the sounds of oncoming traffic. I didn't need to play music, I was engulfed in it. The dashing yellow and white lines on the road provided a rhythm so cerebral that I felt as if my mind was directly plugged into everything around me.

Hot coffee kept me alive, kept me jazzed, always wondering what was next. Tell, Telling Told, I told everyone I saw that they could touch the hem of my robe and feed off of me if they desired. I could feel the electrical cord plugged into their brains, feeding off of mine. I took a gulp of my coffee, this impressed them. If I could have, I would have cracked open my skull and poured the hot coffee directly onto my brain as that would surely impress anyone. I repeated this meet and greet over and over again, welcoming drivers and passengers alike to hug me and hug my mind, and they did, over and over again.

Some of them even high-fived my brain,
that was intense. Drive, driving, driven,
drove, now focused and driving south,
always south. I peered up at the now
exquisitely pitch black sky bursting with
little flashlights. I rolled the driver's
window further down, turning up the
volume on my roadway symphony. I
curved my head out the window, to get a
clearer look at the stars. I was so high on
coffee that I could've counted every star in
the sky and still had time for a smoke break.
Now I have nothing but time, the fun is
over, I'm going to be alive tomorrow, and
the day after and the day after that. What
a bunch of crap! Now I'm just some loser.
Just like yesterday, and the day before,
and the day before that. Why did tonight

feel so special? My thermos and my gas tank were both piping hot and half full. The night was still there in front of me, and even the stars weren't done with me yet, as they needed to be counted, and I needed them to light my way. I felt like a small sun was heating my body from within the car, no light, just heat, and all the people in the streets were planets, and I was a comet, racing away to another orbit. Clearly this had to be the reason. My car was a spaceship, my rocket fuel in my thermos. The roadway symphony started blaring into my ears and into my head again. I was driving fast now, I was in a rush, I knew the direction to go and I knew I would meet someone at my destination – the Tulip Nymph.

The interior of my car filled with a green rotting mist, then blue syrup, then I lit up like a star, filling the inside of the car with a vibrant white light, and my mind opened. It was dry, open, windswept and autumn and full of electricity, my handkerchief was a message, just as sure as I knew there'd be something to read on it, there was. The grime from my face formed a penteract on the cloth, and an arrow circling it, that arrow was ME! It was at that moment that I knew I could do anything, anything in the world. Nothing in site except lighted billboards telling me how to spend my money and see, seeing, saw, and far away refracted sky light from the next town. I finished off the last of the coffee and started walking into the desert.

Once again I felt like I had all the time in the world.

So I started counting every star in the sky, and I was finished before dawn.

# THE RUSSIAN CRATER

My eyes opened, I woke up still in the desert, pre-dawn, the sky was painted in 3 colors-black, blue and red. All the stars were in the blackness, and of course, I knew them all. There was nothing to guide me except just walking toward the noises I heard ahead, like industrial sounds, men working, building or demolishing something. As I started walking toward the sounds, the air became dry, dryer than even a desert should be.

I could feel static charge shooting out from my ears and my shoulders. I guess that should have scared me, but it didn't.

What did scare me was the sky, which, horizon to horizon, turned a pale blood red, chasing away the cooling blue and awe-filled starlit sky. There were no more stars, no more wind. I came upon a place that was strange to me, a rocky edge of what seemed to be a mile wide crater, and at the lower surface were trucks, and bulldozers, and loaders and workmen, all keeping busy, all speaking some kind of Slavic, like Russian. There were piles and piles of junk cars, littering the outer rim of the crater. No one was even acknowledging my presence. Workers with hard hats, flannel shirts and steel-toed boots made their way past me, speaking Russian, streaming chrome, laughing from their faces. Spontaneously, I grabbed one of them by the arm, and asked him where I was, demanding to know, he just blandly looked

away, but did show me his watch, a
digital, it read 3:34 a.m., I assumed a.m..
I looked around, they were piling junk cars
everywhere, making small mountains out
of them. Everyone seemed to be in good
spirits considering it was the middle of a
red sky night and they were piling junk
cars at the bottom of a huge crater. My
body was spinning, the Russians, they were
all dancing and shaking their fists at the
sky, suddenly a distant bell chimed and the
dancing worker bees buzzed away. After
they left, I had synesthesia, and it tasted
like moldy cement and stone and green grit.
I raced away. I started to feel tingly on
the right side of my body, head to toe,
I collapsed, then everything went black,
and I was gone.

# RECHARGE

I woke up walking, the desert was gone,
I was walking beneath the raping sun.
Looking around, it was summer, parks with
merry-go-rounds and dandelions and red
metal peeking up from the grass.
Strangely, I didn't want any food, like
even if a buffet were placed in front of me,
I would leave it alone. I could smell, but
I don't think I could taste, I couldn't even
remember ever having eaten before, not one
memory. The sun was high, it was mid-
day, it was so warm, I was wearing my
sweat, when a trio of Pleiadian stalkers
started waving to me from across the street,
like they knew me. I waved back, and as

I did, my stomach felt warm, like the one who waved just telepathically fed me. They took me by the arm, all smiling, walking me around the corner. They were all sun drenched, both by the sun and by their appearance, their skin was natural and windswept. As we were walking, I felt so good inside, like their smiles were charging my batteries. They brought me to a gas station, then around the corner to the side of the building. There was nothing there except a red brick wall. I looked to them for a cue as to what to do. They started laying down with their feet against the brick wall, and they were all holding hands, they motioned me to join them, so I did. We clasped hands and smiled together, we were in tune. Every copper wire in our blood was sparking and spiking and glowing. I never felt so good in my life. We stared at each other while we were charging, that's what I called it, I think that's what we were doing. They smiled at me, ear to ear, and I smiled back. I loved them all like they were my brothers and sisters, sliding around like snakes, wanting to join with everything and everything with them. I looked up, gazed up, it was night now, the stars were beaming and I felt overdosed with happiness, they understood, and let me go. They released, and my hands felt numb—they felt alone. I wanted to hug god, I wanted to hug god with my brain, I waved goodbye to them, I waved goodbye with my brain. The sparks arched away

from my head and flew onto their
shoulders, where they were absorbed. I
needed to get back to the desert, the road, the
tires turning. Could they help? I asked
them, they nodded, then they poured a red
and purple molten soup onto the road in
front of me, it had screws and nuts in it,
and dirt, but the flow started from their
shoulders. I knew it, this was their way of
brainstorming. All the possibilities they
gave me could have taken me a thousand
lifetimes and a million bodies to fulfill. But
instead, I just told them with my mind that
I needed to get back to my car, and they
understood. The soup stopped flowing, in
fact, it dried up, they seemed sad that it
did. Perhaps I asked too much. I'll never
know, but once the soup dried, they started

rolling together on the ground in symmetry with each other, smiling and humming at the tops of their lungs, and staring at me with a hysterical focus I cannot fully describe. Their hands interlocked, they were forming a circuit to store and then release their energy onto me. This wasn't sadness, this wasn't goodbye, it was their transport, for me. Not only were they humming, but the sky started screaming, all muttering and high pitched pleads, even the clouds raced away like frightened cats. Then the blue sky retreated and was overtaken with a deep somber redness and dusty dark blueness, and stars, a million stars, farm-fresh and hung just for me. I looked back down, and all I saw was sand, but my car was nowhere to be found.

Instead, I saw 16 red steel beams shooting out of the desert floor. They were arranged in a circle, of course, with just enough room for me to fit thru. I slide thru, I slunk thru, as if forces were watching me, and all the while not knowing where they would take me next.

As soon as I reached the center of the circle, the ground felt solid. I felt a buzzing, like a malfunctioning fluorescent bulb. Everything around me, including me, was adorned with an electric blue aura. The buzzing got louder, and invaded my mind, it awoke sleeping strangers and tightened my inner nerves. Bright, brighter, clear brightness, the beams were glowing, clear, then red, then syrupy blue, then clear again, and a little yellow. I began to hear numbers in my mind, numbers, letters, numbers letters, over and over again, something sounded familiar...

and then I remembered why, and god hugged me.

Dies diei eructat uerbum
Numerus
Mensura
Pondus
Ponderibus librata suis
Cl. Ptolem.

# BUBBLES

Bubbles, slimy bubbles joining and merging
with one another in a sickly grotesque way,
then the smell of copper and iron filled my
mouth, then the bubbles began merging with
me, I was surrounded, not bubbles of soap,
or ash, but of triangles, I can't explain it, but
they were triangles, 3 dimensional, like a
pyramid, but with only 3 corners, like a
tetrahedron. They were digging into me
like grains of sand, pressing thru my pours.
All this, the lights, the bright beaming beams,
they kept buzzing, I couldn't take it
anymore. I dropped to the ground and
cried out.....and then all at once my cry
echoed alone. I crouched and cried and

screamed more, even though it all stopped, it was total silence for just a moment, then there was room for ambiance to welcome it's way back in, and I did welcome it. My mind was clear once again, the barn doors were open, everything was clear and windy and dry, no water, no glowing yellow hallways, no coldness. I lifted my head, and saw concrete. 16 red steel beams on asphalt, 16 beams arranged in a circle again, and I was standing in the middle. All the beams were red, shiny, I ran from the beams, and the circuit was complete.

# THE FINAL RUN
## TO THE
## TULIP NYMPH

I ran for miles, past cities, past towns, past glowing skies of spinning circles and wheels and ropes of copper and wicker and groups of solemn watchers, solemnly watching me. I ran a million miles, or so it felt. I ran past the 4th dimension and back to the 3rd, time stretched, then snapped back.....and my feet never touched the ground. I needed to find the Tulip Nymph, but I found myself back on the highway again instead, a full tank of gas and a full thermos of coffee, still heading south, black ash started snowing all around me, and the sun was fractured, forever.

Ash is snowing all around me, do you see the sun? Its sick and fractured. The city is burning, the mall is destroyed, a new home to the new surfers. They burn long angry fires and tires and pile old rusty cement and crumbs of their lives and defend their families within the gutted frame. The air is thick with dust and orbs and light peaking around the red metal. Walking thru the corridors of the mall, I see the rubble and I smell the bonfires, and I see the poor and dying people huddling for warmth, I cannot save them now.

I need to find the Tulip Nymph.

In a dark space minded with smoke and mirrors just past the fountain of joy, the empty fountain,

I see her, the Tulip Nymph, in all her glory. She is bruised and stunned, but I can save her soul. I WILL save her soul! I carefully hold her fragile pale naked body in my hands, thin, longing, gazing at her, gazing at me, my eyes and my senses are invaded, euphoria is in my hands. Dew and ash are holding on to her, but her eyes are waxing warm and bright. Clutching her soft frame, we escape the mall, the war, the crumbling walls of indifference, we escape thru the path of rotting blackberry vines all the way to the rainbow garden.

There, in the garden, we rest under the healing glowing passage tree , we join, and we love and I make love to her body, and she makes love to mine, because she deserves it... and so do I.

# FIREFLY

I see you, but you can't see me. Little firefly flying through the sky, over the rusty fence and into a garden in my backyard. Light up the world little firefly, and play with the air and swish and dart around. I can see you, and I'll stay here with you. It's getting cold and I'll watch over you until the dawn lights turn on. Then where will you go? Will you find a warm leaf and pull it over you to keep you safe, and sleep the day away? Will you change into a fountain and give water to all your friends? I hope you stay alive until tomorrow night, and the night after, and after. I wonder how long you can stay here? Do you see me? I'd like to be your friend. I wish we could be friends. I would let you rest on my arm, and you can look up at me and see me. Are you friends with the ladybugs and the grasshoppers? If you get lonely, say hi to me, I'll be here all night, little firefly.

# YOUR PILLS

Purple trees and stony rocks on rolling grassy hills, puffy little satin bags are where I hide my pills, struggling struggling, holding you down and putting you away, because I know I'll need you on another day. Sleep Sleep Sleep from underneath my bed, and keep me darkest company all whirled up in my head. My mind is a flowery closet and the wood is growing mold, I need a little sunshine before I get too old, sleep sleep sleep in the corner of my room, I wish you would read to me, and tell me stories of my doom. Grow little trees from the floor and blossoms from the shade, and prepare to see the vision in my mind that I have made.

Goodbye goodbye goodbye from my soul
will you depart, after all your pills have
made their way into my heart.

# STARLIGHT

Your words are like swords and my path
is poisoned. I slipped into the morning dew
and I absorbed all of my reflections, my
starlight is waning and I'm afraid it's
dying. My starlight through the cold air is
flying and flying, and you can't see any of
it. But I can see my own breath. The
starlight is mapping my view, carving
valleys of quartz and rivers of fire. I can
hear my heart walking with me through the
dusky forest, and I feel the caressing
leaves, caressing me. Slowly I walk
through a scattered fiery blue tunnel of
moonlight, counting every beam and every
shadow and the tree roots groan with
passion as I step over them on my way

toward the lunar, toward the Moon.
Fussing and glowing warm, covering
everything with life. Watching the Moon
warming me, warming me, leading me on,
leading me around the trees and onto the
hilly, grassy earth, and if darkness is a field,
I am the scarecrow.

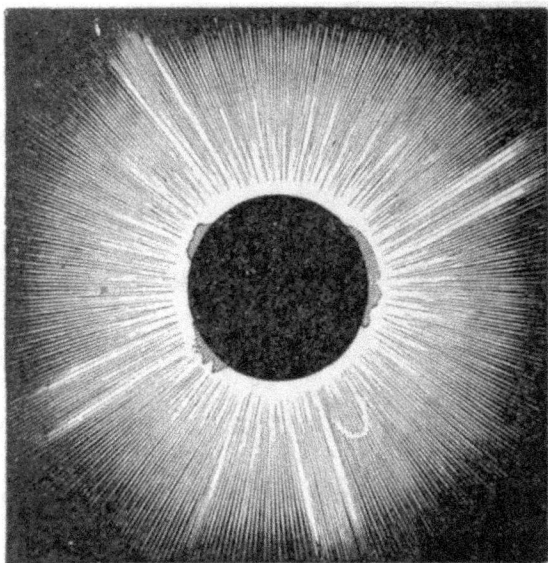

# TIME REDUX

Help, helping, helper, crushing thru the splintery doorway, I can't escape this horrible trail that I've carved, every right turn only traps me more tightly. Nothing illuminating in my mind except the flame of my own selfishness. My life is suffocating me, all at once. Help me, helping me, Helped me. I'm solid in a dark room, I can barely move. The air is dark and smoky and I can't see anything except 16 corners and I also see me. I see me in the room, but I'm born and dying and the room is flooded with time. I can watch from a short distance in empathy, but then I rest and sleep and dream.....dream, dreaming, dreamer, dreamt. I can smell wine barrels rotting in the barn, and rusty beams of iron encircling a body.....somebody.

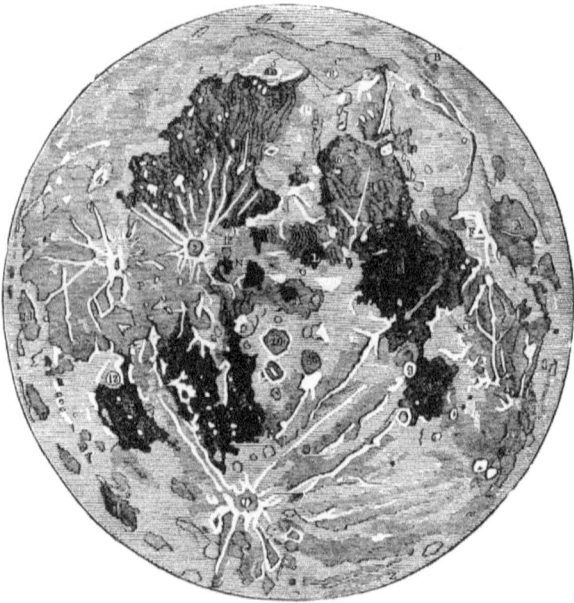

# THE INNER EYE SPY AND THE
## COSMIC EULOGY FOR PAUL

I spy with my inner eye, my consciousness, the one hovering between the serpent and the rainbow. The one sitting lotus style under the orange-creamsicle sky, in the middle of the night, and it's still glowing, giving me a spiritual tan, how tan-talizing. It's the 4th of July, always, every night, without end and the streets and green bridges of my mind are packed with seers and talkers and bloated bohemian bitches with their portable poodles and potent potables. They drape themselves in tightly woven untold lies and thicketed rooted robes, all showing off their faux-regal stature.

I hear with my ears the trodding sounds of lamenting lingerers and sour sojourners zombie-walking their way into the scented meat grinder, they throw themselves willingly into the gears. It's been real, it's been fun, but now, they are done.

I feel everything, I feel you, do you feel me? No... of course you don't. You are truly a busy soul, and I'm sorry that I haven't pulled the knife from your chest, but honestly, I just haven't found the time.

Now I feel responsible for all this, but you wanted it this way, but now look at you, you were wrong. My god is a drunk god, and you were wrong.

Don't worry, don't rush, this world will end, and it's a blessing, but no need to rush, no need to take the bullet train out of town.

I cannot deal with the torturous isles and highway miles and death and decay without you. Where have all my friends gone, where have you gone? Did you ever care much for me?

I know you were always out there in the pointed sandy trenches and stringing the Christmas lights and finding time to find the air to find the energy to find yourself through those tough years. I just wish you would have let us in on your discovery, instead of secreting it away and taking it with you.

You were drowning in love, not misery, couldn't you tell the difference?

I think back to the gray and dark winter months and the concrete walls you gated up around you, only escaping when we jumped over to shortcut our way to every bar, any bar, to hook up and hook in and lament, and do it so damn well.

It was a simpler time. It was a better world, we want that world back, we want you back, we want you to suffocate in your aura, we want your soul back, and even if I have to pry into the shadow world to find it, I will.

If you start to feel queasy, just relax, it's just me crossing over, I'm coming to get you, you needn't fear, you're not alone, you never were alone.

I can't leave you on the other side, it's not right, I can do this, I can find you, for my god is surely a drunk god, so he won't even notice.

Follow close, so no one gets left behind.
Dream if you will, with me, and stream
down onto the astral waterfall, so I can
float with you and find you and bring you
back home.

I froze my body in a cold trance, my wax
peeled away, my skin, my flesh, until only
my soul remained, and without warning, I
was covered by an ocean of fireflies,
thousands of them, they hummed and
bonded to me, and bonded to my soul, and
lifted me up to the lunar, the Moon.
I passed people I knew and cats I've
loved and orange radios I've lost, they all
remembered me, but I floated past them all,
past the flickering drifting space lights and
porous nebulas and glowing rivers of

charged particles, particularly strange, definitely beautiful. Angels and shadow people caressed me and wrapped themselves around me, and they wept with me, about you, they too knew your friends and those who loved you, and they grieve at the waste of genius, the utter waste of genius.......and after the fireflies landed me on the gravely Moon, they dispersed, they reversed and faded away.

Lying on the dust of the Moon, I asked god to show me your soul, and he laughed, god laughed at me and staggered away, he hated me, he loved me, he wanted me to kill him, and I pushed him away, I pushed her away, I slept, I slept a day, then a night, and then I begged to visit the other side of the Moon, the other side of reality, and god smiled and opened a path of radiant light, diamonds shining, making the path on the Moon glow. And I followed it, and I followed it into a rocky cave of teeth and poison, then a tunnel of deep blue and sharp ice. I wandered for what seemed like forever. Lost in the tunnels of the Moon, I am alive, I feel everything, the tunnels connect me with every soul, alive and dead, and I was thrust into a crowded room, a party, Christmas lights hanging, everyone breathing smoke and carbon and glass. Everyone kept pushing and shoving and hugging me with their arms and screaming at me with their faces, their mouths on fire, their smiling grins dragging across my face like chalk, and then my brain folded in on itself, or so it felt, and

I collapsed, and the party raged on all around me, and my soul dissolved and scattered into the air, where everyone breathed me in, and they choked on me. Their luxurious hands grasping their throats as I leaked out of their mouths and onto the floor, then eternity looked at me in the face, and for a moment, I was everywhere, doing everything, but only for a moment, then the party was over, then love touched my soul, my life force. I blacked out. I found myself lying in a field of juniper and golden-seal and golden zeal, under a tweed sky. Find, finding, found!... I found you in that field, strolling across some old railroad tracks and the rust from the beams flew up and clung to you, and you embraced it and slunk along and surried

down to the grass, and made snow angels
out of the dust of life, and rust of death, and
the bark and blood of this dimension, and it
was surreal and at the same time I had to
look away. I could only see your
resolutions, your confirmations, your
footnotes, and your hastily planned escape
plan. You smiled, you seemed happy,
finally letting the light in. You asked me to
make snow angels with you, so I did, and
our arms passed each other as we outlined
our wings, always coming close but never
touching, but I had to connect to you, to
reach you, to rescue you.

I couldn't wait another second, so without
warning, I reached and grasped your hand,
ice cold and I was warming you, and the
sun screamed, and the air froze into an

infinite number of cubes, and you looked at me with horror, your eyes longing and your mouth quivering. Finally you're scared, why weren't you scared before? Why didn't you scare us more, why couldn't you just stay? We stayed locked together for a moment, but then our circuit tripped and our planes rumbled away from each other, I felt your hand still, but I couldn't see you, but I could feel you. And I found myself back in my body, back on earth, back from the Moon, and slowly slipping out of my trance. Just then it started raining, and the drops tasted like the ocean, like tears, like you missed us. And the rain was a hello from another plane of existence, the only hello that we're allowed.

We'll take it, we'll take anything from You,
and we'll absorb it into us and make clocks
and alarms and shakers and buzzers and
bright lamps out of our memories of You.

# JESUS AND JOANIE

Jesus and Joanie are gonna visit and play checkers and drink gin and root beer with us all, and we can all stare at your paneling and jest at your stunningly appointed visuals and the dusty brass knuckles and your mountains of circles of emotion and shock and awe. Joanie and Jesus always stayed too late and we were grateful for it, so let's have a toast to the most and peace to some and war to others and rest for you now, now, now, we all can fall asleep, together.

# THE BLUE COLLAR BUDDHA

I'm a liar, I'm a liar, I'm a liar. I am the
Blue Collar Buddha. I am your boss's
boss's boss, but I am also just like the rest of
you average Joes. I put my Shakti on one
Chakra at a time.

And I would rather fornicate with the
truth, than marry the lie.

Verily, all who hear my voice, and see my
aura, mark me well, a pound of happiness
weighs more than a pound of success.

Curse the winged angels of death, die
blackbirds die!

Three of them circle above me, one with a
blueish white aura, they swim in a sky
crowded with purple and white clouds, but

I turn from them, I want to arrive alive, and so I run from the blackbirds who are swarming around like fireflies. I want to arrive alive, where the blackbirds can taste my flesh and brag of my divinity. But time in the present is a roaring fire, and so I must abide there for now, and if ego is a corn stalk, then I am a field.

The three blackbirds are trying to whisper something to me, but I can't understand them, so I kneel down to hear, and they rattle off a series of letters and numbers, but their voices come out in a warbly errant tone, like a bad AM radio station. One of the birds reaches into their wing and holds out a handkerchief toward me, white and dry, the wind plays it a bit. Another blackbird motions that I should take it.

So I do. I think that's what they want me
to do. I try to give it back, but they motion
that I can keep it. I thank them, and then
I motion my mind to my sky and I fly off
onto my way.

My body was spinning with honey and
dandelions, and my car turned into a gothic
fireplace, roaring with ancient tales.

I spotted a spirit whom I knew, flying
further up the sky-way and then the
highway, and I flashed my orange and
green aura to insist to her to pull over her
spaceship and park in my dimension.
My protege, my blazing star. She was
crying, her tears weren't drying, and she
was in a hurry.

So without a word I tossed her the
handkerchief so she could dry her eyes, but
she let her tears fall anyways, only wiping
the lava and dust from her face. Then I
realized, she was searching too. Aren't we
all? She spent some time explaining her
journey, and her trials and her tribulations,
and her hazy manifestations. Heavy stuff,
but she was tough, so I knew she would
stay lit up. We hugged and said our
goodbyes, but we knew we'd meet again.
Her eyes beamed with determination as
she became her star and drove away. The
gravel from the road swirling up from her
tires like a dusty ball of flames.
As her star slowly disappeared into the
asphalt horizon, I laid down on some tall
grass near a large boulder which needed

my company. Everything felt so heavy, so
meaningful. Everything felt so finished
and tearful. And then the door slowly
closed shut on my life.........

and then, another...opened.

# INSTRUCTIONS FOR MAKING COMETS

In my spare time I build and supply comets to this and several other star systems.

Comets are made up of ice and dirt and nuts and bolts don't you know?

They weigh about the size of a small house, if that house had iron radiators and a cement foundation. If that house had a one car garage and a finished basement, with a fireplace.

Yes, that's about the weight of a comet.

Comets are made in the Pleiades system and are sent out everywhere in the universe for decoration and because we all need a little dirty ice sometimes.

They are constructed in large wooden and wicker warehouses on the largest planet orbiting Taygeta.

Making comets is a messy business and not very profitable, and so the ice water that is trucked in from that planet's moon must be dehydrated to reduce the cost of transport, morphine is used for this purpose. Once the ice water makes it to the warehouse it is stored in one of a series of tanker fields where it waits to be reconstituted before being pumped into the comet extruder. The inhabitants of the planet are very nervous coffee drinkers and very critical and suspicious of celestial manufacturing and so they are often seen spying thru the factory windows to watch the comets as they are being fabricated. They are pacified by drinking the morphine laced ice water which they siphon from the storage tanks. In fact, it is not uncommon to see roaming mobs of morphine addicted teens looking for trouble near the outskirts of the industrial zone, where the methane monoliths live.

Each comet contains approximately 800 pounds of iron wing nuts, and 300 pounds of scrap sheet metal, and 3 tons of crushed ice. This combination is mixed with 5 tons of Georgia red clay and some sand from the coast of Maine before being spun into the various shapes comets tend to be seen in. Once the comet is spun, it is launched from the outdoor finishing platform with a spring-loaded mass object sling (MOS), the slings are about 500 yards long and use launching ties made from recycled tires.

These comet factories can be refitted to produce asteroids, however, with the demand for asteroids being low and the cost of retooling the factory quite high, as well as the 3-6 months of down-time necessary to complete the refit, that makes asteroid manufacturing more of a niche market.

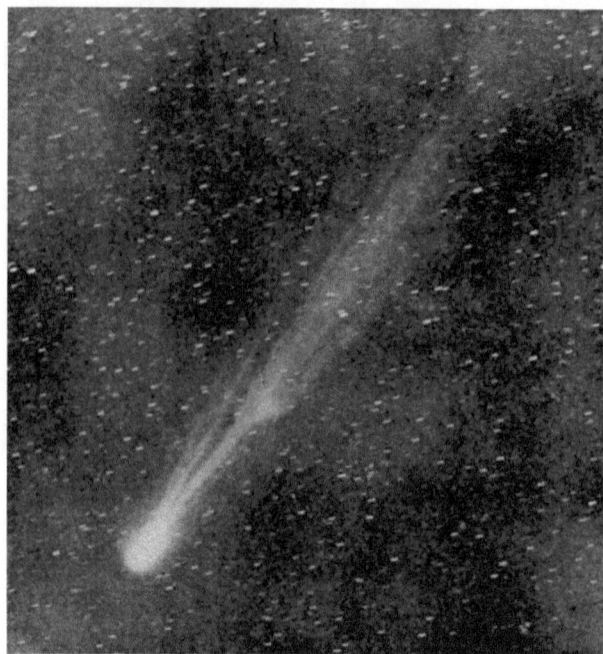

The end.